Unlock Your Guide To Profitable Home Sales

Jerry Sun
Unlock Your Guide To Profitable Home Sales
Sell your home for Top and FAST Dollar

Published by BooxAi
ISBN: 978-965-578-768-9

Unlock Your Guide To Profitable Home Sales

Sell your home for Top and FAST Dollar

Jerry Sun

Contents

About the Author

Jerry Sun, a seasoned real estate agent with over two decades of experience, shares insider strategies in 'Maximize Your Home Sales.' This comprehensive guide emphasizes strategic selling, offering invaluable insights to empower sellers and achieve top-dollar sales.

Introduction

Welcome to "Maximize Your Home Sales: A Comprehensive Guide to Sell Your Home for Fast and Top Dollar"! In the pages that follow, I, Jerry Sun, a seasoned real estate agent with over two decades of experience, will be sharing the insider secrets and strategies crucial for maximizing the value of your most valuable asset – your home.

In the world of real estate, where every decision counts, selling a home isn't merely a transaction; it's a strategic process that can significantly impact your financial well-being. Understanding the nuances of presenting and marketing your home correctly can lead to not just a swift sale but also securing the best highest value so you can utilize your net proceeds.

Why This Book Matters

Your home isn't just a space, place, or thing; it's your most valuable asset, potentially it can generate passive income or serving as a tool to hedge against inflation. Knowing how to position and market your property effectively and maximize your assets can make all the difference.

Have you ever wondered if your real estate agent is employing every available tactic to maximize your home's value? This guide will equip you with insights and knowledge to navigate the selling process confidently, allowing you to collaborate more effectively with your chosen agent or perhaps even take the lead yourself, ultimately aiming to achieve your mutual goal: maximizing your asset, leading to increased financial gain.

Bibliography
My Experience and Credentials

As a testament to my dedication and expertise in real estate, I've garnered numerous accolades and achievements over the years:

Recipient of prestigious awards like the RE/MAX Multi-Million Dollar Producer Top Agent, RE/MAX Diamond Club, and RE/MAX Titan Club awards, placing me among the top echelons of RE/MAX agents worldwide.

Inducted into the RE/MAX Hall of Fame and honored with the Lifetime Achievement Award for my exceptional contributions to the field.

Recognized by esteemed publications such as the Los Angeles Times, Taiwan Daily Newspaper, and World Journey Newspaper for my insights and expertise in real estate.

Earned the highest reviews and customer ratification on prominent platforms such as Yelp, Zillow, Google, Realtor.com, and various other websites. These positive reviews stand as a testament to my commitment to delivering exceptional results and client satisfaction.

Leveraging my comprehensive education—a Bachelor of Science from the University of Southern California (USC). I've honed my skills and knowledge to provide unparalleled service to my clients.

My name is Jerry Sun, and with over 20+ years in the real estate industry, I've navigated market fluctuations, evolving trends, and diverse client needs. Through this book, I aim to empower you with the tools and industry's insider's know-how to achieve the best possible outcome in selling your home.

Let's embark on this journey together, my goal is to share these invaluable strategies and insights garnered from my extensive experience to help you sell your home for Top and FAST Dollar as this book cover has proclaimed.

Chapter 1
Understanding Your Local Real Estate Market and House Value

Before diving into selling your home, it's crucial to grasp the pulse of your local real estate market. This step sets the stage for effective sales strategies and offers a realistic view of your home's current value.

Think of selling your home as embarking on a journey ahead. Like any journey, knowing your starting point and the destination ahead is essential.

As a resident, you possess unique insights into your community that real estate agents might not fully grasp. Free online resources like Zillow.com, Redfin.com, and realtor.com offer valuable information that can empower you with expertise akin to a certified appraiser or realtor.

The most common way of determining your house value is a CMA "Comparable Marketing Analysis" report.

A CMA (Comparative Market Analysis) report in real estate is a comprehensive analysis that helps determine the value of a property by comparing it to similar properties that have recently sold or are currently on the market in the same area. Real estate agents or appraisers usually prepare CMAs to assist sellers in setting a competitive price for their property or to aid buyers in making informed offers.

In a CMA report, includes details such as:

1. Comparable Properties - Recently sold (within 0-3 months) properties similar in size, condition, location, and features to the subject property.

2. Current Listings - Properties that are currently on the market that are competing with the subject property.

3. Adjustments - Any variations between the subject property and the comparable properties, such as differences in square footage, number of bedrooms or bathrooms, upgrades, or lot size, which might affect the property's value.

e.g. Ocean view, mountain view, additional parking garage/spaces, new flooring, new kitchen, new bathroom, new roof and etc.

4. Market Trends - Analysis of the current real estate market conditions and trends in the area.

By examining the above mentioned data and facts, a CMA report can helps both buyers and sellers understand the current market value of a property. For sellers, it aids in setting a reasonable listing price, while for buyers, it assists in making informed offers based on the market value of similar properties.

Below, you'll find a sample chart that illustrates as an example. The following sample chart can serve as a snapshot of current market conditions, helping you gauge your home's potential value within this landscape.

Comparable Marketing Analysis

Describe the condition of the project and quality of construction.

Describe the common elements and recreational facilities.

Are any common elements leased to or by the Homeowners' Association? ☐ Yes ☐ No If Yes, describe the rental terms and options.

Is the project subject to a ground rent? ☐ Yes ☐ No If Yes, $ ______ per year (describe terms and conditions)

Are the parking facilities adequate for the project size and type? ☐ Yes ☐ No If No, describe and comment on the effect on value and marketability.

HOA Fees Charge $ ______ per month X 12 = $ ______ per year

Utilities included in the unit monthly assessment ☐ None ☐ Heat ☐ Air Conditioning ☐ Electricity ☐ Gas ☐ Water ☐ Sewer ☐ Cable ☐ Other (describe)

General Description	Interior materials/condition	Amenities	Appliances	Car Storage
Floor #	Floors	☐ Fireplace(s) #	☐ Refrigerator	☐ None
# of Levels	Walls	☐ WoodStove(s) #	☐ Range/Oven	☐ Garage ☐ Covered ☐ Open
Heating Type Fuel	Trim/Finish	☐ Deck/Patio	☐ Disp ☐ Microwave	# of Cars
☐ Central AC ☐ Individual AC	Bath Wainscot	☐ Porch/Balcony	☐ Dishwasher	☐ Assigned ☐ Owned
☐ Other (describe)	Doors	☐ Other	☐ Washer/Dryer	Parking Space #

Finished area **above** grade contains: ______ Rooms ______ Bedrooms ______ Bath(s) ______ Square Feet of Gross Living Area Above Grade

Are the heating and cooling for the individual units separately metered? ☐ Yes ☐ No If No, describe and comment on compatibility to other projects in the market area.

Additional features (special energy efficient items, etc.)

Describe the condition of the property (including needed repairs, deterioration, renovations, remodeling, etc.).

Are there any physical deficiencies or adverse conditions that affect the livability, soundness, or structural integrity of the property? ☐ Yes ☐ No If Yes, describe

Does the property generally conform to the neighborhood (functional utility, style, condition, use, construction, etc.)? ☐ Yes ☐ No If No, describe

Comparable Marketing Analysis

There are ________ comparable properties currently offered for sale in the subject neighborhood ranging in price from $ ________ to $ ________

There are ________ comparable sales in the subject neighborhood within the past twelve months ranging in sale price from $ ________ to $ ________

SALES COMPARISON APPROACH

FEATURE	SUBJECT	COMPARABLE SALE # 1		COMPARABLE SALE # 2		COMPARABLE SALE # 3	
Address and Unit #							
Project Name and Phase							
Proximity to Subject							
Sale Price	$						
Sale Price/Gross Liv. Area	$ sq. ft.						
Data Source(s)							
Verification Source(s)							
VALUE ADJUSTMENTS	DESCRIPTION	DESCRIPTION	+ (-) $ Adjustment	DESCRIPTION	+ (-) $ Adjustment	DESCRIPTION	+ (-) $ Adjustment
Sales or Financing Concessions							
Date of Sale/Time							
Location							
Leasehold/Fee Simple							
HOA Mo. Assessment							
Common Elements and Rec. Facilities							
Floor Location							
View							
Design (Style)							
Quality of Construction							
Actual Age							
Condition							
Above Grade Room Count	Total / Bdrms. / Baths	Total / Bdrms / Baths		Total / Bdrms. / Baths	0	Total / Bdrms. / Baths	
Gross Living Area	sq. ft.	sq. ft.		sq. ft.	0	sq. ft.	
Basement & Finished Rooms Below Grade							
Functional Utility							
Heating/Cooling							
Energy Efficient Items							
Garage/Carport							
Porch/Patio/Deck							
Net Adjustment (Total)		☐ + ☐ -	$	☐ + ☐ -	$ 0	☐ + ☐ -	$
Adjusted Sale Price of Comparables		Net Adj. % Gross Adj. %	$	Net Adj. 0.0 % Gross Adj. 0.0 %	$	Net Adj. % Gross Adj. %	$

Summary of Sales Comparison Approach

____

____

____

____

____

____

____

____

____

____

Indicated Value by Sales Comparison Approach (Approx.) $

Chapter 2
Preparing Your Home for Sale
Enhancing Your Home's Value through Smart Preparations

This process can be very exciting, but it's important to maintain a balanced approach. Remember, making wise investments in your home can significantly increase its appeal to potential buyers. You will never have a second chance to make your FIRST impression.

Your goal is to generate lots of foot traffic and attract offers (or as many offers) as quickly as you can. Picture shopping for something you really desire, like a car or a valuable piece of jewellery at a store. If you've been eyeing the exact same item for 8+ weeks (2 months), your reaction might involve trying to negotiate a better deal, testing if the seller is eager to accept your offer.

The longer your home stays on the market, the more it could work against you. Prospective buyers might begin to suspect issues with the property, impacting their interest.

Here are the **7 Steps** on Preparing Your Home for Sale prior to putting it up on the Market.

1. Identify Repairs and Plan:

- **Interior Assessment:** Walk through each room noting necessary repairs caused by regular wear and tear. Look for wall damages, flooring issues (cracks, chips), and problems in the kitchen and bathrooms. Additionally, inspect the ceiling or walls for hairline cracks caused by settling.
- **Kitchen and Bathrooms:** Check appliances for proper functioning, inspect cabinets for water damage, ensure sinks and faucets works with no leaks, and evaluate flooring conditions.
- **Systems Check:** Verify HVAC and water heater functionality, test smoke/carbon monoxide detectors, and labeled each electrical breaker for code compliance.
- **Repairs vs. Upgrades:** Differentiate between essential repairs to maintain value and upgrades that add value to your property.
- **Exterior and Yard Inspection:** Assess the structural integrity of garage doors, exterior doors, roofs, eaves, drainage, and foundations. Check decks, landscaping, and fences for any damages or required maintenance. Also make sure there are no peeling paint, wood rot on the roof eaves and etc.

2. Declutter and Clean for Spaciousness:

- **Organizing Spaces:** Systematically declutter all areas, using storage bins and compartments to maintain tidiness. Deep clean the house to restore carpets and overall cleanliness.

- **Professional Cleaning Services:** Consider hiring cleaning professionals for thorough and efficient cleaning, including deep carpet cleaning or restoration.
- **Enhancing Appeal:** A well-maintained and clean home often attracts higher offers and garners better attention from potential buyers.

3. Depersonalize Your Home:

- **Neutralizing Space:** Remove personal items such as family photos, collectibles, or personal belongings to create a neutral environment that allows potential buyers to visualize themselves living in the space.
- **Creating a Blank Canvas:** This step helps potential buyers focus on the property itself rather than the current owner's personal style or lifestyle choices.

4. Strategic Painting:

- **Fresh Paint:** Apply fresh paint where needed, particularly focusing on areas that may show signs of wear and tear or outdated color schemes.
- **Color Choice:** Opt for light neutral colors (e.g. Swiss coffee or egg shell white) recommended by experts as they appeal to a wider range of potential buyers, aiding in easier visualization of their own belongings in the space.

5. Home Staging for Appeal:

- **Creating an Emotional Connection:** Stage your home to evoke positive emotions and connections with potential buyers. This helps in setting your home apart and generating more interest.

- **Added Value:** Staged homes tend to sell faster and sometimes at higher prices than non-staged properties, making staging a worthwhile investment.

Staging your home plays a crucial role in the sales process. It capitalizes on the human tendency to make emotional decisions and then rationalize them logically. The ultimate aim is to make an impeccable first impression that ensures your home stands out to potential buyers.

Statistics from Realtor.com indicate that, on average, staged homes tend to sell a whopping 88% faster and for around 20% more than those that aren't staged. This data underscores the significant impact staging can have on attracting buyers and increasing the perceived value of your property. By strategically setting up and presenting your home, you're effectively influencing the emotional connection potential buyers develop, which ultimately contributes to a faster sale and potentially higher offers.

6. Maintain Consistency:

- **Routine Maintenance:** After preparing your home for sale, maintaining its pristine condition is crucial. Establish a routine cleaning schedule involving everyone in the household to ensure quick readiness for any last-minute showing requests.
- **Exterior Maintenance:** Regularly maintain the exterior, including lawn care, porch upkeep, and keeping the property accessible and tidy.

7. Pre-showing Checklist:

- **Final Touches:** Before each show, perform a thorough check for cleanliness and tidiness, including spot-cleaning surfaces, ensuring proper lighting, and creating a welcoming ambiance with soft music or open curtains.

Here's a checklist you can use before showing:

- Quickly check rooms for any clutter or dirt
- Vacuum or sweep the floors
- Wipe down sinks and faucets in the bathrooms and kitchen before showing
- Clean kitchen countertops
- Empty the trash bins
- Secure your valuable belongings
- Put away pet dishes (if any)
- Sweep your front porch or entryway
- Open all curtains and shades for natural light
- Turn on all lights to brighten the space
- Consider playing soft music for a welcoming atmosphere
- Consider putting air freshener in living room area
- Set A/C or Heater thermostat to a comfortable temperatures

Following these 7 detailed steps can significantly enhance your home's presentation, appeal to potential buyers, and potentially increase your chances of receiving higher offers.

We've included a sample "Pre-Listing Check List" for your reference.

Chapter 3
Marketing Strategies
The 4P's - Product, Price, Place, and Promotion

Back in the 1950s, Harvard professor Neil Borden introduced the marketing mix, later known as the four P's. In his 1964 article, "The Concept of the Marketing Mix, "The 4P's " showcased how companies could use advertising strategies to connect effectively with consumers.

These four P's serve as pillar for your marketing strategy. Each P plays a crucial role, and they often intertwine in practical applications.

Let's explore these 4Ps—product, price, place, and promotion—specifically in the context of real estate marketing:

1. Product: In real estate, the "product" isn't just the physical house; it's the entire package—the location, features, and lifestyle it offers. Understanding what makes your property unique helps in highlighting its strengths to potential buyers.

2. Price: Setting the right price is key. It's not just about the value of the property but also about how it aligns with market trends and buyer expectations. Pricing too high can deter buyers, while pricing too low might possibly undervalue your asset.

3. Place: Where and what place do I advertise?

Strategic placement of your property in listings is crucial. Ensure your listing reaches potential buyers by featuring it prominently on high-traffic real estate websites.

4. Promotion: This involves how you market and advertise your property. It's about utilizing various channels & online platforms such as social media to reach potential buyers. Effective promotion highlights the property's strengths and attracts interested parties.

Understanding and effectively utilizing these 4Ps can significantly impact your real estate marketing strategy, helping you position your property optimally in the market and attract the right buyers.

1. Product - The property you are selling is your product - Focus on your Uniqueness and package it well.

Your offering isn't just a "house"; it embodies unique characteristics that will appeal to potential buyers. Every home boasts distinct geographical features, amenities, and conditions. Highlight the aspects of your home that resonate most with the type of buyer you aim to attract. Whether it's a scenic backyard, an ocean or mountain view, a spacious garage, a guest house, or a serene cul-de-sac location—showcase these features. Facilitate potential buyers in envisioning themselves living in and enjoying your property, significantly enhancing your chances of a successful sale.

2. Price - Will my asking price generate a high foot traffic?

Pricing profoundly impacts the speed of a home sale. Initiate by conducting a Comparative Market Analysis (CMA)—an aggregation of recent area sales, as discussed in Chapter 1. Consider leveraging the current market dynamics; for instance, listing your home slightly below the average market price (around 2-3%) can generate multiple offers. Remember, the listing price doesn't necessarily equate to the selling price. Your primary aim is to attract substantial foot traffic, as more visits typically lead to increased offers.

3. Place - Where and How do I advertise?

It's essential to put your property where potential buyers will see it. To reach the right audience, focus on featuring your listing prominently on popular real estate websites. Platforms such as Zillow, Redfin, and Realtor.com attract a large pool of potential buyers. By showcasing your home on these sites, you can expand your reach and connect with over 80+% of potential buyers. This strategic placement boosts the chances of attracting the right people interested in your property.

4. Promotion - How and where do I advertise my product?

When it comes to promoting your property, your toolbox is diverse: think flyers, social media, open houses, emails, real estate websites, and more. The goal is to cast a wide net, reaching as many people as possible to find the perfect buyer for your property.

But there's a secret weapon in this arsenal: a dedicated landing website. This page is key. You must attract off potential buyer into this landing page.

Here's what you should consider on your landing page it includes:

- Professional photos of both the exterior and interior (think Photoshop enhancements for that extra polish).

- Drone footage offering a unique aerial view.

- Detailed 2D and 3D floor plans for a comprehensive understanding of the space.

- Immersive 3D walkthroughs using platforms like Matterport.

- Engaging videos showcasing the property.

- In-depth property descriptions that bring its unique aspects to life.

- Highlighted property features that make it stand out.

- Insights into the neighborhood, showcasing what makes the area special.

This landing website becomes your stage to showcase your property in its best light, capturing the attention of potential buyers and giving them an immersive experience that can't be overlooked.

Chapter 4

Navigating the Selling Process
Negotiation Tactics: Strategies for Handling Offers and Negotiating Effectively

Mastering the art of negotiation as a seller can be complex. Questions about effective negotiation, setting the right asking price, and deciding on compromises can be overwhelming. However, the following real estate negotiation tips can help you to simplify this process.

1. Hiring a Real Estate Agent

Engaging a real estate agent is a key to negotiation strategy. Their market expertise, objectivity, and ability to secure the best deal are invaluable. For sale by owner might seem enticing, but homeowners often feel overwhelmed by the complexities. Expertise in legal intricacies is crucial. Even if you contemplate an independent sale, consulting with a real estate agent can kick-start the process.

2. Set a Realistic Asking Price

Setting a realistic asking price slightly below average is crucial. Overpricing can discourage potential buyers and ultimately cost you more. Evaluate the local market and your home's value.

Highlight unique features; if your home offers more (e.g. ocean view, pool, guest house and etc.), a slightly higher price is reasonable. Keep in mind, an overpriced listing might inadvertently make your competitors' properties appear more appealing.

3. Control your Emotion / Maintain Politeness and Courtesy

Irrespective of your price point (aka low ball offers) or sales approach, maintaining courteous conduct towards potential buyers is crucial. Rudeness can disrupt negotiations. Remember, people buy emotionally and justify it logically.

Effective communication, positive interactions, and prompt responses create a win-win situation for everyone.

4. Conduct Home and Termite Inspections

A comprehensive home and termite inspection are crucial. Identifying issues enables you to rectify them or adjust the listing price accordingly. Addressing these problems or making improvements can potentially boost your home's value. It also serves as an "expectation" that gives potential buyers confidence in the home's condition.

5. Offer to Cover Closing Costs

When dealing with demanding buyers or negotiations, covering closing costs can be persuasive. This gesture, encompassing appraisal and escrow fees, facilitates a smoother sale and may boost the overall sale price.

6. Implement Review Offer Deadlines

Setting a Review Offer day creates urgency, hinting at multiple offers. Typically within 7-10 days of listing or after the first week of open house, this strategy prompts action and urgency to potential buyer.

Establishing an expiration date on your counteroffer during negotiations sets a buyer deadline. This will also prevents prolonged negotiations and allows exploration of other potential buyers if the initial offer falls short.

7. Don't Hesitate to Reject Offers

Rejecting offers that don't align with your requirements is acceptable and legal. Accepting a subpar offer often leads to regrets. Ensure any offer benefits you the highest; rejecting it without a counteroffer leaves room for potentially better offers.

8. Don't SHOW your card

Think of real estate negotiation as a poker game. Refrain from sharing personal stress or urgency with potential buyers, as they might use this information against you. Maintaining discretion strengthens your negotiating position. Keeping your cards close ensures a stronger negotiating position.

9. Have your Seller's Disclosures ready

Under your state's real estate disclosure laws, many things require disclosure. These may include deaths on the property, roof leaks, lead-based paint (federal law), known toxins, current insurance claim and water damage. This list may vary by state; research and consult your agent to ascertain other necessary disclosures!

Negotiation in home sales is challenging, demanding your best self. If you need help negotiating your home's value, your real estate agent can offer invaluable guidance.

Chapter 5
Frequently Asked Questions Before Listing Your Home for Sale & when you have an Accepted Offer

Selling a home brings up lots of questions, just like buying one does. Whether you're new to this or have done it before, selling a home can feel unfamiliar. That's because it's not something most people do everyday, and the rules and ways of doing things can change a quiet bit.

Before you even start selling your home, questions start popping up. It's smart to be ready and understand how things work. One great way to get ready is by asking questions.

There's a wonderful truth that applies to everyone: there really aren't any silly or foolish questions. Asking questions is an essential part of learning and growing. It's through asking that we gain new knowledge, broaden our understanding, and find solutions. Each question, no matter how simple it may seem, is an opportunity to expand our insights and become more knowledgeable. So, never hesitate to ask because that's how we all progress and become better at what we do.

Here are the top frequently asked questions that home sellers ask before listing a home for sale, questions relating to house value & pricing, contracts, and questions relating to purchase offers.

Frequently Asked Questions Before Listing Your Home For Sale

1. When's the best time to sell my home?

It's a big question, but the answer isn't the same everywhere. Each area has its own real estate rhythm.

Usually, spring works well in many spots. But selling time varies by location. Take California, for example. June and May stand out there. June means better prices—around $21,000 more than the yearly average! And in May, homes fly off the market, about 8 days quicker than usual.

But remember, it's different for every place. Your Realtor knows the deal in your area. They'll help pinpoint the best time for your home sale, considering all the numbers and specifics. Because everyone's situation is different, chatting with your Realtor will help nail down the perfect timing for you.

2. How's the real estate market right now?

Before putting their home up for sale, many sellers wonder about the local real estate scene. A top Realtor should be able to give you lots of info about the market to explain how things are going. One of the key things to look at is the ***"average days homes"*** stay on the market. This can show sellers how fast homes are selling once they're up for sale.

There are more indicators your Realtor might share before you list your home, like market absorption rates, the number of homes sold in a month compared to previous years, average sale prices, and how close sale prices are to the listing prices. These stats can paint a picture of the market conditions for sellers.

3. What steps should I take to prepare my home for sale?

Before listing your home, there are essential things to consider we have discussed about this in Chapter 2.

Check out the checklist provided in this book. Making a good first impression is crucial when selling a home. You want your home to shine and show its best side.

Not properly preparing a home for sale can put a home owner at a huge disadvantage.

4. What should I disclose to potential buyers when selling my home?

It's crucial to be upfront about any known issues or defects in your home. Being honest about problems with the roof, appliances, or any part of the house is essential. If you're aware of issues, it's best to fix them before listing your home. This helps prevent complications, potential lawsuits, or problems that could arise during inspections or even after selling the house.

Laws about seller disclosures vary by state, but beyond the legal requirements, it's a good idea to share everything you know with potential buyers.

You don't have to go hunting for problems to disclose, but if you're aware of something not caught by the home inspector, it's best to tell your buyer.

Here are some key things to always disclose:

- Environmental concerns like lead paint, asbestos, radon, or mold.
- Pest issues, especially termites or carpenter ants.
- Natural risks such as flood zones or drainage problems.
- Construction flaws or system issues like electrical or plumbing.
- Details about HOA rules or property boundary disputes.
- Death on the property.
- Roof leak
- Sewer / Drainage problem

5. How much is my home worth?

Many times, people inflate the price of what they think their house is worth based on their personal perspective. However, it is important to try and keep your own opinion to yourself when determining how much your house is actually worth.

The amount your house is worth depends on multiple factors including its size and the neighbourhood. To get a good idea of how much your house is worth, you should compare it to similar houses in your area. There are also helpful home evaluation tools to use online. Simply type in your address and it will track your home value.

6. How can I set a competitive yet reasonable price for my home?

Determining the right price for a property involves a nuanced analysis that incorporates both objective and subjective elements. Conducting a comparative market analysis (CMA) allows sellers to assess recent comparable sales, active listings, and market trends in their neighbourhood. Evaluating the property's unique features, condition, amenities, and positioning it against similar properties helps in setting a competitive price. Collaborating with a knowledgeable real estate agent adept at interpreting market data and understanding buyer psychology aids in accurately pricing the property to attract potential buyers while maximizing its value.

7. Why is my Tax assessed value different than what you say my home is worth?

Why is my tax-assessed value different from what you claim my home is worth? Assessed value doesn't equate to market or appraised value. Many homes sell for significantly more or less than their assessed value. The assessed value, used for property tax purposes in your local area, is multiplied by the tax rate to calculate yearly taxes. However, it doesn't reflect what your home might fetch in the market.

Some buyers mistakenly think that a home listed above its assessed value is overpriced, which isn't accurate. Similarly, they might suspect something's wrong if the list price is far below the property tax assessed value. In reality, the assessed value doesn't dictate your home's actual worth to potential buyers. Some home-owners overlook their assessed value, only to realize their local authorities have gradually increased it over the years, despite the market value remaining stagnant.

8. What is the difference between a list price and sale price?

This common question has a straightforward answer. The list price is what a home is currently listed for sale at, while the sale price is what it's sold for.

How does one figure out a home's value? Realtors use various methods, with the most common being a comparative market analysis (CMA). This analysis dives into recently sold similar homes in the past 3-6 months. Although a CMA doesn't predict the exact sale price, a top Realtor's analysis should significantly narrow down the price range.

A well-done CMA considers multiple aspects beyond just the home itself, including the local area and neighbourhood. Factors involved in a professional CMA include square footage, bedroom and bathroom count, kitchen upgrades, window quality, roof age, lot characteristics, location (whether it's on a main street or in a neighbourhood), style of the home, and flooring type.

A professionally completed "CMA" will take into account many features of not only a home, but also the local area and neighbourhood. Considerations that a professionally completed "CMA" include, but is not limited to:

- Square footage
- Number of bedrooms
- Number of bathrooms
- Upgrades to kitchen
- Window quality
- Roof age
- Lot features
- Location; primary or neighbourhood street?
- Style of residence
- Flooring type

9. Can I determine how much my home is worth from an internet website?

The answer to this frequently asked question is NO! Anyone who has bought a home, sold a home, or just browsing for homes on websites such as Zillow, Trulia, realtor.com and etc. . These are also commonly referred to as third party real estate websites. Third party real estate websites are not local to every real estate market.

While these Third party internet websites can provide estimates of a home's value, they often use automated valuation models (AVMs) or algorithms based on public data and may not capture the full picture. These estimates can sometimes be inaccurate due to limited information on a specific property's unique features, upgrades, or local market conditions. For a more accurate valuation, it's recommended to consult with a real estate professional who can perform a comprehensive analysis considering various factors beyond what these websites can provide.

10 . Should I price my home higher to leave room for negotiations?

Pricing a home higher to leave room for negotiation might seem like a good strategy, but it can have drawbacks. While the idea is to start higher and then negotiate down, it can actually deter buyers. Many people search for homes within specific price ranges, and if your home is priced too high, it might not even show up in their search results. This means fewer buyers might even consider your home, reducing the chances of getting offers.

A better approach is to set a price slightly lower than your competitors reflecting on your home's value based on the current market. This can attract more potential buyers, generate more interest, and sometimes even lead to multiple offers. When buyers see a home priced fairly, they're more likely to consider it seriously, and this can give you better negotiating power. You might end up with competing offers, allowing you to negotiate from a stronger position without needing to start with a higher price.

11. Is it worth upgrading your house before selling?

Selling a house is a big deal, and your main goal might be getting the most money for it. Not every home needs fixes before selling, but it's important to check if any repairs or upgrades are needed. Deciding to renovate before selling depends on things like how old the home is, its condition, and where it's located.

Deciding to renovate before selling isn't always straightforward. You want to make as much money as possible, but not every renovation will add the same value. Choosing the right renovations can save you time and might even increase how much money you make.

Before you start fixing things up, let's talk about the kinds of updates you might think about and when it might be okay to sell a house without doing any remodelling.

Here are some renovations and repairs that, according to research, can add the most value to your home:

- **Garage Door Replacement:** Seems simple, but it can give a great return. A new, practical, and attractive garage door can make a lasting impression on potential buyers.
- **New Exterior Siding**: Replacing outdated siding can impress buyers. Choosing options like stone veneer, vinyl, or fiber-cement siding can help recover your costs.
- **A Fresh Coat Of Paint**: Painting your home in neutral colors can unify its look. It's an affordable way to give your home a fresh feel and increase its value.
- **Upgraded HVAC**: If your system is old or broken, updating it can be attractive to buyers who want energy-efficient homes.

- **Energy-Efficient Windows**: Replacing old or broken windows can save on energy bills and sometimes even qualify for tax credits. Options like vinyl or wood windows are popular.
- **Roof Replacement**: Though not the first thing you'd consider, a new roof can significantly impact your home's value and won't go unnoticed.
- **Kitchen Remodel**: Consider smaller changes like replacing appliances, updating fixtures, or refinishing countertops and cupboards. Stick to classic options to appeal to more buyers.
- **Bathroom Remodel:** A midrange remodel with functional updates like replacing fixtures or adding new tiles can make financial sense compared to high-end luxury remodels.

12. Should I include Appliances?

Deciding whether to include appliances or keep them negotiable when selling a home depends on your preferences and the market dynamics. Here are the key points to consider:

Including Appliances:

Pros:

1. Attractiveness - Including appliances can make your home more appealing to buyers, especially for those seeking move-in ready homes.

2. Competitive Edge - It can give your listing a competitive edge in a market where similar homes don't offer appliances.

3. Simplicity - It simplifies the process for buyers who might not want the hassle of buying appliances separately.

Cons:

1. Reduced Negotiation - Buyers might expect a lower sale price if appliances are included that is NOT up to their taste or outdated.

2. Potential Wear and Tear - Appliances might wear out or break down over time, leading to additional maintenance costs for you before the sale.

Leaving Appliances as Negotiable:

Pros:

1. Flexibility - Keeping appliances negotiable allows you to use them as leverage during negotiations or as incentives for buyers.

2. Higher Sale Price - You might have the opportunity to sell appliances separately for additional profit.

3. Personal Preference - Some sellers prefer taking their appliances to their new home or have sentimental attachment to certain items.

Cons:

1. Reduced Attractiveness - For some buyers, the absence of included appliances might make your home less appealing or require additional expenses after purchase.

2. Complication - Negotiating appliances separately can complicate the buying process and might deter some buyers.

Ultimately, consider your priorities, the local market trends, and the preferences of potential buyers in your decision. Consulting with a real estate agent can offer valuable insights into what's common and advantageous in your specific market.

13. How will a realtor market my home?

You should expect a thorough marketing plan from your Realtor when selling your home. Just putting up a sign and waiting isn't the approach anymore. Nowadays, it's crucial to reach buyers through both traditional methods like newspapers and mailings, as well as online platforms.

A good Realtor should have a solid website, a helpful real estate blog, and an active presence on social media. It's essential that a Realtor's website ranks high in search results because more than 90% of buyers start their home search online! This online exposure is key to reaching potential buyers.

Frequently Asked Questions when you have an Accepted Offer....

1. What negotiation strategies should I be aware of when receiving offers

1. Negotiation plays a vital role in selling your home. Familiarizing yourself with different negotiation strategies can empower you to handle offers more effectively. Stay receptive to negotiations, weighing factors like the offer price, contingencies, closing dates, financing terms, and any special requests from the buyer.
2. Leverage the expertise of your real estate agent in negotiations. They bring invaluable insight to evaluate offers, counteroffers, and ultimately arrive at a mutually beneficial agreement. Their guidance helps align your objectives with the buyer's needs, facilitating a successful transaction. Being flexible and open-minded

during negotiations can lead to a deal that satisfies both your goals and the buyer's requirements.

2. What Are Common Repairs Required by Banks?

When a buyer seeks financing from a bank for a home purchase, the bank conducts an appraisal. During this appraisal, the appraiser looks for safety concerns or hazards. In the buyer's purchase offer, they often specify an amount for which the seller is responsible to cover for necessary repairs outlined by the bank. These repairs usually involve addressing safety issues identified by the appraiser. Common bank-required repairs might include installing missing handrails, fixing broken windows, addressing peeling paint, replacing missing electrical covers, and repairing severely deteriorated roofs. These repairs are typically aimed at ensuring the safety and habitability of the property for the buyer.

3. What happens if the appraised value comes in is lower than contracture purchase price?

Apart from ensuring a home is safe, the bank's appraiser checks if its value aligns with the buyer-seller agreement. However, there are times when these values don't quite match up. Here's a closer look at the possible scenarios:

a) Seller Makes a Concession - This is a common response to a low appraisal. The seller might need to agree to sell the home at the appraised value, even if it's lower than what was initially agreed upon. It's a compromise where the seller accepts a reduced price to move forward with the sale.

b) Buyer Bridges the Gap - In some instances, the buyer might opt to cover the difference between the purchase price and the appraised value out of their pocket. However, this is quite rare because most buyers find it challenging to pay more for a home than what the bank values it at.

c) Transaction Cancellation - Unfortunately, this is a common outcome when a property's appraised value falls short. If the buyer isn't willing to pay more than the appraised value and the seller won't adjust the price, the deal might fall through, leaving both parties disappointed.

d) Challenging the Appraisal - Contesting an appraisal is a complex process. It requires substantial evidence and careful consideration. Changing the appraised value is difficult unless there's concrete and persuasive information supporting the challenge. It's a route that's challenging to navigate and doesn't always yield a favorable outcome.

4. What is a "sale contingency" or "subject to buyer selling their existing home"?

When buying a home, some buyers prefer to secure a suitable property before selling their current one. This strategy involves a sale contingency, a term commonly seen in purchase offers. Essentially, a sale contingency means that the potential buyer can only proceed with purchasing the "new" home after successfully selling their existing home.

This contingency allows the buyer some flexibility in the home-buying process. It offers a safety net, ensuring they secure a new home but only if they can successfully sell their current property first. This condition safeguards the buyer from owning two homes simultaneously or getting financially stretched between the old and new properties. However, it could potentially delay the seller's plans if the buyer's home sale process takes longer than expected.

5. What is an Inspection Contingency?

Inspections serve as crucial safeguards in a home purchase, often included as contingencies in buyer's offers. These contingencies grant buyers the right to conduct various inspections and tests to ensure the property meets their expectations and standards.

Buyers typically shoulder the expenses involved in conducting inspections. These examinations can encompass a wide array of assessments, ranging from structural inspections to assessments of electrical, plumbing, and roofing systems. Additionally, tests for pests, radon, mold, and other environmental concerns may also be part of the inspection process.

Buyers usually have a specified period, often a few days, to complete these inspections. During this time, they meticulously assess the property's condition and any potential issues. Following the inspections, buyers typically have an additional set number of days to decide whether to waive the inspection contingencies or request the seller to address any findings from the inspections.

These contingencies serve as a crucial protection mechanism for buyers, offering them the opportunity to investigate the property thoroughly before committing to the purchase. It allows them to make informed decisions based on the property's actual condition while having the option to negotiate repairs or walk away if significant issues arise during the inspection period.

6. What is a Loan Contingency?

A loan contingency, when selling your home, is a clause often included in the contract that protects the buyer. It stipulates that the sale of the property is dependent on the buyer securing financing or a mortgage within a specified period.

For the buyer, this contingency allows them time to apply for a loan and obtain approval. If, for some reason, they are unable to secure financing within the agreed-upon timeframe, this clause allows them to withdraw from the contract without facing penalties or losing their earnest money deposit.

From the seller's perspective, a loan contingency means that while the buyer secures financing, there's a level of uncertainty until the loan is fully approved. If the buyer fails to secure a loan within the specified period and decides to withdraw from the purchase, the seller needs to relist the property and restart the selling process.

This contingency helps protect both parties, providing the buyer with an opportunity to secure financing while allowing the seller to keep the property on the market if the sale falls through due to loan approval issues.

Chapter 6
Frequently Asked Questions on Listing Agreement

1. How long does the listing agreement last?

The length of a listing agreement, the contract between you and your real estate agent, isn't the same for everyone. Each agent has their own preference when it comes to how long they want the agreement to last. This means there's no one-size-fits-all answer to this common question.

One key thing to think about is how long houses typically take to sell in your area. If most homes are on the market for around 70 days before they're sold, having a listing agreement for just 90 days might not give enough time to attract the right buyer. It's like matching the agreement length to the pace of the market so that you have a better chance of selling your home within that time frame.

2. How much commission do you charge?

The commission charged by a Realtor is something that can be negotiated. Don't believe anyone who tells you otherwise. However, there's a wise saying in real estate that often holds true:

"You get what you pay for." If a Realtor is offering a lower commission rate, it's essential to consider if they'll be as dedicated in negotiating for your best deal. Think of it this way: if you were paid less for doing the same job, would you put in the same effort? Most likely not.

Selecting a Realtor purely because they offer the lowest commission rate can sometimes be a common mistake made by home sellers. While aiming to save money is understandable, it's crucial to consider the value and effort a Realtor brings to the table. Sometimes, choosing an agent solely based on a lower commission might mean getting a reduced level of service or dedication to securing the best outcome for your property sale.

3. What happens if I'm not happy and want to cancel the contract?

When selling a home, people don't usually like to think about what happens if they're "unhappy" and want to cancel the contract. But sometimes, this question comes up. Everyone wishes for a quick sale at a great price, but it doesn't always happen that way. Each state and contract has its own rules, but typically, if you decide to cancel the listing agreement, you might be responsible for covering any expenses the real estate agent or their brokerage incurred while working on selling your home.

Chapter 7

Other Miscellaneous Frequently Asked Questions At or After Closing

1. What are the common closing expenses for home sellers?

Common closing expenses for home sellers typically include:

- **Real Estate Commission** - This fee is usually the most significant expense, covering the compensation for both the seller's and buyer's agents.
- **Title Insurance** - Sellers often pay for the buyer's title insurance policy, ensuring a clear title transfer to the new owner.
- **Property Taxes** - Sellers might need to cover property taxes accrued up to the closing date.
- **Transfer Taxes or Recording Fees** - These charges vary by location and cover the costs of transferring property ownership legally.
- **Escrow or Attorney Fees** - Charges for escrow services or legal representation during the closing process.

- **Home Warranty** - Some sellers opt to provide a home warranty to the buyer as an added incentive, covering certain repairs or replacements of home systems or appliances.
- **Unpaid Homeowners Association (HOA) Fees** - If applicable, sellers might need to settle any outstanding HOA dues up to the closing date.
- **Repairs or Credits** - Agreed-upon repairs or credits to the buyer might also be included in the closing expenses.

These expenses can vary based on the location, specific agreements between the buyer and seller, and negotiations during the closing process. Consulting with a real estate professional can provide a more accurate estimation of closing costs in your situation.

2. Why isn't anyone interested or look at my home?

Understanding Why Your Home Isn't Getting Attention. It's a common concern: "Why isn't anyone interested in my home?" This question often involves multiple factors influencing buyer interest. While several reasons might contribute, one prominent issue often revolves around the asking price.

a) Pricing - A home priced too high can steer potential buyers away. Buyers tend to compare multiple homes, and if they perceive a property as overpriced, they're more inclined to explore other options within their budget. This might mean they find another suitable home before even considering yours.

b) Curb Appeal - First impressions matter. A poorly maintained exterior or unattractive curb appeal can deter buyers from exploring further. If your home lacks visual appeal from the outside, buyers might overlook it altogether.

c) Location Concerns - The location of your home can also impact its visibility. Factors like proximity to amenities, schools, public transportation, or neighbourhood safety significantly influence a buyer's interest.

d) Marketing Strategies - Effective marketing is crucial. If your Realtor's marketing efforts aren't reaching the right audience or highlighting your home's unique features, it can hinder interest. This includes online presence, photography quality, and showcasing the property's strengths.

Understanding these potential reasons can guide you in addressing the issue. Consider re-evaluating the pricing strategy, enhancing your home's curb appeal, discussing marketing strategies with your Realtor, or exploring ways to highlight the positives of your home's location to attract more potential buyers.

3. How frequently and by which methods should a realtor be communicate with home sellers?

The frequency and ways your Realtor communicates can differ among agents. Generally, you should anticipate hearing from your Realtor at least once a week when selling your home. However, these communication methods may vary based on what suits you best.

a) Frequency of Contact - Typically, expect updates from your Realtor once a week. This ensures you're regularly informed about your home's status, potential offers, or any market changes affecting your property.

b) Tailored Communication - Your Realtor should adapt to how you prefer to communicate. If you like emails, your Realtor should reach out via email. Likewise, if you prefer text messages, phone calls, or face-to-face meetings, your Realtor should accommodate those preferences. This personalized approach helps ensure clear and comfortable communication between you and your Realtor.

By adjusting their communication methods to match your preferences, your Realtor can ensure that you feel involved and well-informed throughout the selling process. This tailored approach aims to create a more positive and collaborative selling experience for you.

4. Should I be present during showings at my home?

It's an easy one – no! There are several reasons why sellers should avoid being present during showings. The primary reason? Potential buyers might feel uneasy discussing your home openly with their Realtor if you're around. They might hold back from saying anything that could unintentionally offend you as the seller.

The best approach is to leave shortly before the scheduled showing and return after you're sure the buyer and their Realtor have left your home. This gives buyers the freedom to explore your home openly and share their honest thoughts without any discomfort.

5. Do open houses really work?

Open houses stir a bit of controversy in the real estate realm. Some Realtors may assure sellers that holding open houses every weekend will sell their home. However, this claim might not entirely reflect reality.

The truth? Open houses aren't a necessity to sell a home. Often, Realtors advocate for them to attract additional buyers. However, less than 5% of homes actually sell due to open houses.

When discussing this with your Realtor, it's essential to gauge their stance on open houses. Make sure you're comfortable with their response. Being aligned with your Realtor on the importance of open houses ensures you're both on the same page regarding their role in selling your home.

5. How do I prepare my home before showing?

The following check list for your reference before showing:

- Quickly check rooms for any clutter or dirt
- Vacuum or sweep the floors
- Wipe down sinks and faucets in the bathrooms and kitchen before showing
- Clean kitchen countertops
- Empty the trash bins
- Secure your valuable belongings
- Put away pet dishes (if any)
- Sweep your front porch or entryway
- Open all curtains and shades for natural light
- Turn on all lights to brighten the space
- Consider playing soft music for a welcoming atmosphere
- Consider putting air freshener in living room area
- Set A/C or Heater thermostat to a comfortable temperatures

 # Pre-listing Checklist

To get the best return on your home, it's essential to enhance its appearance.
Here's the checklist to guide you through the process.

LIVING ROOM

Clean and dust all surfaces and shelves

Vacuum upholstery and drapes

Replace worn cushions and carpets

Arrange furniture for a spacious and inviting feel

Ensure proper lighting, replace bulbs if needed

Add fresh decor touches

KITCHEN

Deep clean all cabinet fronts

Ensure all appliances are working

Deep clean appliances surfaces

Minimize items on counter display

All cabinet & drawers doors open/close smoothly

Remove refrigerator magnets, Hide trash can

BEDROOM

Put fresh bedding and pillows

Clean shades and curtains

Organize the room or remove excess furniture

Remove family or personal photos

Dust and organize nightstands

Declutter and organize items in closets

BATHROOM

Eliminate all odors and use air freshener

Clean toilet seats and bowl

Clean shower, sink, tub, and wall stains

Ensure all appliances are working

Place worn rugs and towels

Minimize items on vanity display

LAUNDRY ROOM

Clean all surfaces

Organize shelves and cabinets

Wipe the washer and dryer

Put all clothing away

DINING ROOM

Clean surfaces, dining table and chairs

Organize cabinets

Declutter the dining table and surrounding areas

Check and clean light fixtures

BASEMENT

Clean water heater and drains

Change furnace filter

Organize items and remove clutter

Clean and paint the walls & floor

DEN / OFFICE

Organize books, files, and items on shelves

Dust and clean all surfaces, shelves, and desks

Check and clean electronic devices and cords

Minimize items on the desk

Pre-listing Checklist

To get the best return on your home, it's essential to enhance its appearance.
Here's the checklist to guide you through the process.

GARAGE

- Organize to create floor space
- Organize items in bins or shelves
- Cover exposed wiring for safety
- Ensure the garage door is working
- Sweep or clean the garage floor
- Organize tools and equipment

CURL APPEAL

- Mow the lawn
- Trim trees and shrubs
- Remove weeds from flowerbeds
- Clean the patio and outdoor furniture
- Clean or repaint the front door
- Power wash the exterior if needed

INTERIOR

- Repaint with neutral colors if needed
- Clean all blinds and curtains
- Mop all wood flooringand tile floors
- Deep clean the rugs or carpet floors
- Clean windows and window walls
- Repair holes or cracks in walls
- Clean baseboards and trim
- Check and replace lightbulbs
- Dust all lights and ceiling fans
- Fix anything not working properly
- Remove family and personal photos
- Organize to free up space, minimize items display
- Eliminate all odors; light a candle for an aroma
- Take out all trash, hide kids' toys, and pets' toys

EXTERIOR

- Fill in driveway cracks and walls
- Wash and clean windows
- Clean and repair gutters
- Ensure all outdoor lights are working
- Clean or paint mailbox
- Clean pool, filters, and plumbing
- Replace missing shingles
- Repair shutters and screens
- Refinish steps and porch
- Sweep driveway clear of leaves
- Make sure doorbell is working
- Check if home alarm is functioning
- Hide the trash bin somewhere invisible
- Do not park cars in the driveway

Conclusion

Your Home Sale Journey

Congratulations on reaching the end of Unlock Your Guide to Profitable Home Sales Guide. Your dedication to this guide shows your commitment to securing the best outcome for selling your home.

Selling your home isn't just about transactions; it's about the memories, dreams, and hopes nurtured within those walls. I hope this guide has provided you with valuable insights and strategies to confidently navigate the selling process.

Your home holds a wealth of personal stories—it's been a shelter, witnessed your cherished moments, and fostered your dreams. As you embark on this journey, trust in the knowledge you've gained in this guide and in your decisions.

I want to express my heartfelt gratitude for choosing this guide. Your dedication to maximizing your home sale for the best outcome is truly commendable.

Now, let's take this knowledge and determination, step into the next chapter of your life confidently. May your home sale journey bring swift success and fulfillment.

Thank you for allowing me to be a part of your home sale story.

Warm regards,

Jerry Sun - Broker Associate

BRE#01338788